Let's Go Shopping

Pete and Jem are very helpful at the supermarket, but end up causing chaos with a tower of food on display.

Targeting Subject-Verb-Object sentences and the conjunction 'and' for listing, this book provides repeated examples of early developing syntax and morphology which will engage and excite the reader while building pre-literacy skills and making learning fun. It also exposes the reader to multiple models of the target grammar form.

Perfect for a speech and language therapy session, this book is an ideal starting point for targeting client goals and can also be enjoyed at school or at home to reinforce what has been taught in the therapy session.

Jessica Habib studied speech pathology at the University of Sydney, graduating in 2012. She has since worked with children in indigenous health, community, private, not-for-profit and education settings in both Australia and the UK. Jessica loves the privilege she has of seeing children thrive as they are guided to build and strengthen their communication skills.

Carina Ward is an illustrator based in the Blue Mountains, Australia. She works with watercolour and ink to create beautiful, bright images and likes to add a touch of humour to her work. Carina loves the way pictures tell stories and open up imaginary worlds.

T0143321

What's in the pack?

Let's Go Shopping

A *Grammar Tales* Book to Support Grammar and Language Development in Children

Jessica Habib

Illustrated by Carina Ward

Routledge
Taylor & Francis Group

LONDON AND NEW YORK

Cover image: Carina Ward

First published 2023
by Routledge
4 Park Square, Milton Park, Abingdon, Oxon OX14 4RN

and by Routledge
605 Third Avenue, New York, NY 10158

Routledge is an imprint of the Taylor & Francis Group, an informa business

British Library Cataloguing-in-Publication Data
A catalogue record for this book is available from the British Library

Library of Congress Cataloging-in-Publication Data
A catalog record for this book has been requested

ISBN: 978-1-032-27431-7 (pbk)
ISBN: 978-1-003-29272-2 (ebk)

DOI: 10.4324/9781003292722

Typeset in Calibri
by Apex CoVantage, LLC

Let's Go Shopping

We are going shopping.
We are helping Mum and Dad.

I find mangoes and papaya.

You spot apricots and cherries.

I get bread and porridge.

You grab milk and cheese.

I find flour and sugar.

You see spaghetti and rice.

I get toothpaste and shampoo.

You find nappies and wipes.

We see lollies and popcorn.

We like lollies and popcorn.

We want lollies and popcorn.

Uh oh!

I say sorry to
Mum and Dad.

You say sorry to
Mum and Dad.

We say sorry to the lady and man.

We do not get lollies or popcorn!